A Bilingual Guide for Beginners

Introduction

A Bilingual Guide for Beginners

hello/ bonjour

Welcome to this bilingual learning book! Whether you are a beginner in English or French, this book will help you improve your vocabulary, grammar, and conversation skills. Each section provides translations, examples, and exercises to strengthen your understanding.

Chapter 1: Greetings and Basic Phrases

English - French

Hello – Bonjour

Good morning – Bon matin

Good evening – Bonsoir

How are you? – Comment allez-vous ?

I'm fine, thank you – Je vais bien, merci

What is your name? – Comment vous appelez-vous ?

My name is… – Je m'appelle…

Nice to meet you – Enchanté(e)

Goodbye – Au revoir

See you later – À plus tard

Exercise: Practice saying these phrases aloud and write a short dialogue using at least five of them

____

____

____

____

____

____

____

____

Chapter 2: Numbers and Counting

English - French

One – Un

Two – Deux

Three – Trois

Four – Quatre

Five – Cinq

Six – Six

Seven – Sept

Eight – Huit

Nine – Neuf

Ten – Dix

Exercise: Write the numbers 1-10 in French and use them in sentences (e.g., "I have three apples" - "J'ai trois pommes").

Chapter 3: Common Objects and Colors

Objects (English - French)

Book – Livre
Pen – Stylo
Table – Table
Chair – Chaise
Bag – Sac

Colors (English - French)

Red – Rouge
Blue – Bleu
Green – Vert
Yellow – Jaune
Black – Noir

Exercise: Look around you and describe five objects in your room using their colors and names in French.

____

____

____

____

____

____

____

____

Chapter 4: Days of the Week and Months

Days (English - French)

Monday – Lundi

Tuesday – Mardi

Wednesday – Mercredi

Thursday – Jeudi

Friday – Vendredi

Saturday – Samedi

Sunday – Dimanche

Months (English - French)

January – Janvier
February – Février
March – Mars

April – Avril
May – Mai
June – Juin

July – Juillet
August – Août
September – Septembre

October – Octobre
November – Novembre
December – Décembre

Exercise: Write a short paragraph about your favorite day of the week and your birth month.

Chapter 5: Basic Conversations

Example Dialogue

English: A: Hello! How are you?
B: I'm fine, thank you. And you?
A: I'm good too. What is your name?
B: My name is Sarah. Nice to meet you! A: Nice to meet you too!

French:
A: Bonjour ! Comment allez-vous?
B: Je vais bien, merci. Et vous ?
A: Je vais bien aussi. Comment vous appelez-vous ?
B: Je m'appelle Sarah. Enchantée !
A: Enchanté(e) aussi !

Exercise: Create your own conversation and practice with a friend.

Every word you can learn is a key
that opens a new door. Keep
going , you're on the right path!

Chaque mot que tu apprends est
une clé qui ouvre une nouvelle
porte .continue , tu es sur un bon
chemin!

Chapter 6: Family and Relationships

Family Members (English - French)

Father – Père

Mother – Mère

Brother – Frère

Sister – Sœur

Grandfather – Grand-père

Grandmother – Grand-mère

Uncle – Oncle

Aunt – Tante

Cousin – Cousin(e)

Son – Fils

Daughter – Fille

Exercise: Write a short paragraph introducing your family using these words.

Chapter 7: Common Verbs and Sentences

Essential Verbs (English - French)

To be – Être

To have – Avoir

To go – Aller

To do – Faire

To eat – Manger

To drink – Boire

To like – Aimer

To play – Jouer

To speak – Parler

To learn – Apprendre

Example Sentences

I am happy – Je suis heureux/heureuse

She has a cat – Elle a un chat

We go to school – Nous allons à l'école

They play football – Ils jouent au football

Exercise: Write five sentences using these verbs.

Congratulations on completing this bilingual learning guide! Keep practicing daily, and soon, you will be more confident in both English and French. Bonne chance!

Chapter 8: Food and Drinks

Common Foods (English - French)

Bread – Pain

Cheese – Fromage

Meat – Viande

Fish – Poisson

Vegetables – Légumes

Fruits – Fruits
Rice – Riz
Pasta – Pâtes

Drinks (English - French)

Water – Eau

Coffee – Café

Tea – Thé

Juice – Jus

Milk – Lait

Exercise: Describe your favorite meal using at least three of these words.

Chapter 9: Travel and Transportation

Transportation (English - French)

Car – Voiture

Bus – Bus

Train – Train

Bicycle – Vélo

Airplane – Avion

Taxi – Taxi

Example Sentences

I take the bus every day
– Je prends le bus tous les jours

She travels by plane
– Elle voyage en avion

Exercise: Write a short paragraph about a trip you have taken or would like to take.

____

____

____

____

____

____

____

____

Chapter 10: Weather and Seasons

Weather (English - French)

Sun – Soleil

Rain – Pluie

Snow – Neige

Wind – Vent

Cloud – Nuage

Storm – Orage

Seasons (English - French)

Spring – Printemps

Summer – Été

Autumn – Automne

Winter – Hiver

Example Sentences

It is sunny today
– Il fait beau aujourd'hui

In winter, it snows
– En hiver, il neige

Exercise: Describe the weather in your city today using these words.

Chapter 11: Professions and Work

Professions (English - French)

Teacher – Professeur

Doctor – Médecin

Engineer – Ingénieur

Artist – Artiste

Farmer – Agriculteur

Police officer – Policier

Firefighter – Pompier

Writer – Écrivain

Example Sentences

My father is a doctor
– Mon père est médecin

She works as a teacher
– Elle travaille comme
professeur

Exercise: Write a short paragraph about your dream job.
____

____

____

____

____

____

____

____

____

Dialogue 1 : Se présenter
Français :

A : Bonjour ! Je m'appelle Marie. Et toi ?
B : Salut ! Je suis John. Enchanté de te rencontrer.

English:
A: Hello! My name is Marie. What about you?
B: Hi! I'm John. Nice to meet you.

Dialogue 2 : Demander des directions
Français :
A : Excusez-moi, où est la gare ?
B : La gare est à droite, puis tout droit.

English:

A: Excuse me, where is the train station?
B: The train station is to the right, then straight ahead.
Dialogue 3 : Commander au café

Français :
A : Je voudrais un café, s'il vous plaît.
B : Bien sûr ! Vous voulez du sucre ?

English:
A: I would like a coffee, please.
B: Of course! Do you want sugar?

Dialogue 4 : Parler de la météo

Français :
A : Il fait beau aujourd'hui, n'est-ce pas ?
B : Oui, il fait très chaud !

English:
A: It's nice weather today, isn't it?
B: Yes, it's very hot!
Dialogue 5 : Faire des projets

Français :
A : Que fais-tu ce week-end ?
B : Je vais au cinéma. Et toi ?

English:
A: What are you doing this weekend?
B: I'm going to the movies. What about you?

Les Animaux - Animals

1. Je saute et je croasse, qui suis-je ?
I jump and I croak, who am I?
Réponse / Answer : Une grenouille / A frog

2. J'ai des rayures noires et blanches, mais je ne suis pas un cheval. Qui suis-je ?

I have black and white stripes, but I am not a horse. Who am I?

Réponse / Answer : Un zèbre / A zebra

Les Objets - Objects

3. Je brille dans le ciel la nuit, mais je ne suis pas une étoile. Qui suis-je ?

I shine in the sky at night, but I am not a star. Who am I?

Réponse / Answer : La lune / The moon

4. Je suis fait de verre et je t'aide à mieux voir. Qui suis-je ?

I am made of glass and I help you see better. Who am I?

Réponse / Answer : Des lunettes / Glasses

Les Aliments - Food

5. Je suis jaune et courbé, et les singes m'adorent. Qui suis-je ?
I am yellow and curved, and monkeys love me. Who am I?
Réponse / Answer : Une banane / A banana

6. Je suis rond et rouge, et on me trouve souvent dans les salades. Qui suis-je ?
I am round and red, and I am often found in salads. Who am I?
Réponse / Answer : Une tomate / A tomato

STAY STRONG & POWER ON

Bonjour ! - Hello!
Le matin, Emma se réveille
et dit : "Bonjour !" à sa
maman.
In the morning, Emma wakes
up and says: "Hello!" to her
mom.

Sa maman répond : "Bonjour
Emma ! Bien dormi ?"
Her mom answers: "Hello
Emma! Did you sleep well?"

Emma sourit et dit : "Oui, j'ai
fait un joli rêve !"
Emma smiles and says: "Yes,
I had a beautiful dream!"

Le Petit Déjeuner - Breakfast

Emma s'assoit à table. Il y a du pain, du beurre et un verre de lait.
Emma sits at the table. There is bread, butter, and a glass of milk.

Elle dit : "Miam ! J'adore le pain avec du beurre."
She says: "Yummy! I love bread with butter."

Sa maman lui donne une pomme. "Mange aussi un fruit, c'est bon pour la santé !"
Her mom gives her an apple. "Eat a fruit too, it's good for your health!"

Au Parc - At the Park

Après le petit-déjeuner, Emma va
au parc avec son papa.
After breakfast, Emma goes to
the park with her dad.

Elle court et joue sur le toboggan.
"Regarde, papa ! Je glisse vite !"
She runs and plays on the slide.

"Look, Dad! I'm sliding fast!"
Papa applaudit : "Bravo Emma !"
Dad claps: "Well done, Emma!"

Une Surprise - A Surprise

En rentrant du parc, Emma voit un joli ballon rouge dans le jardin.
When coming back from the park, Emma sees a pretty red balloon in the garden.

"Oh ! C'est pour moi ?" demande Emma.
"Oh! Is it for me?" asks Emma.

Maman sourit : "Oui, une surprise pour toi !"
Mom smiles: "Yes, a surprise for you!"

Emma saute de joie et serre le ballon contre elle.
Emma jumps with joy and hugs the balloon.

THINK IT, WANT IT, GET IT

L'Heure du Dodo - Bedtime

Le soir, Emma met son pyjama et prend son doudou.
In the evening, Emma puts on her pajamas and takes her teddy.

Maman lui lit une histoire :
"Bonne nuit, Emma ! Fais de beaux rêves."
Mom reads her a story:
"Good night, Emma! Sweet dreams."

Emma ferme les yeux et s'endort doucement.
Emma closes her eyes and falls asleep gently.

À l'école - At School
Le lendemain matin, Emma se prépare
pour aller à l'école.
The next morning, Emma gets ready to
go to school.

Elle met son sac sur son dos et dit : "Je
suis prête !"
She puts her backpack on and says:
"I'm ready!"

À l'école, la maîtresse dit : "Bonjour les
enfants !"
At school, the teacher says: "Hello,
children!"

Emma lève la main et répond :
"Bonjour, maîtresse !"
Emma raises her hand and replies:
"Hello, teacher!"

Les couleurs - Colors
À l'école, Emma apprend les couleurs.
At school, Emma learns the colors.

Maîtresse : "Quelle couleur est-ce ?"
(elle montre un objet rouge)
Teacher: "What color is this?" (she
shows a red object)

Emma : "Rouge !"
Emma: "Red!"

Maîtresse : "Très bien ! Et cette couleur
?" (elle montre un objet bleu)
Teacher: "Very good! And this color?"
(she shows a blue object)

Emma : "Bleu !"
Emma: "Blue!"

THANK YOU!

MERCI